PETER THE GREAT
and Tsarist Russia

by Miriam Greenblatt

BENCHMARK BOOKS

MARSHALL CAVENDISH
NEW YORK

ACKNOWLEDGMENT

With thanks to W. Bruce Lincoln, Distinguished Research Professor of Russian History, Northern Illinois University, for his helpful reading of the manuscript.

Benchmark Books
Marshall Cavendish Corporation
99 White Plains Road
Tarrytown, New York 10591-9001

© Marshall Cavendish Corporation 2000

Library of Congress Cataloging-in-Publication Data
Greenblatt, Miriam.
Peter the Great and Tsarist Russia / by Miriam Greenblatt.
p. cm.—(Rulers and their times)
Includes bibliographical references and index.
Summary: Describes the life and times of Peter the Great, the tsar who transformed Russia, and includes poems, legends, and diary excerpts.
ISBN 0-7614-0914-9
1. Peter I, Emperor of Russia, 1672–1725.—Juvenile literature. 2. Russia—Kings and rulers—Biography—Juvenile literature. 3. Russia—History—Peter I, 1689–1725—Juvenile literature.
4. Russia—Social life and customs—1533-1917—Juvenile literature. 5. Russia—History—To 1533—Sources—Juvenile literature. 6. Russia—History—1613-1917—Sources—Juvenile literature.
I. Title. II. Series.
DK131.G74   1999   947'.05—dc21   98-25656   CIP   AC

Printed in Hong Kong
1 3 5 6 4 2

Picture research by Linda Sykes, Hilton Head, SC

Photo Credits
Cover: Superstock [detail]; page 5: Superstock; pages 6, 26, 57, 63: Tretyakov Gallery, Moscow/Bridgeman Art Library; pages 9, 11: Stock Montage; page 10: Castle Howard Estate, York, England; pages 14, 20, 41, 46, 54: North Wind Picture Archives; pages 29, 32: Hermitage, St. Petersburg/Scala/Art Resource; page 19: Michael Holford; pages 23, 35: Sovfoto/Eastfoto; pages 38, 49: Russian State Museum, St. Petersburg/AKG, London; page 45: Recklinghausen, Ikonenmuseum/AKG, London; page 52: AKG, London; pages 53, 73: Tretyakov Gallery, Moscow/AKG, London; page 59: Private Collection/Bridgeman Art Library; page 64: V.I. Lenin State Library, Moscow/Bridgeman Art Library; page 69: Museum of History, Novgorod/Laurie Platt Winfrey Inc.

Contents

A World Apart

By the end of the seventeenth century, western Europe was well on its way to becoming a modern society. Although most people were farmers, an ever-increasing number were earning their living through manufacture, trade, and banking. Literacy was no longer limited to members of the clergy. Interest in science was growing, and technology was making rapid strides. Fleets carrying goods and people sailed to the Americas, the Far East, and Africa.

Russia, in contrast, was a world apart. It had no fleet, few schools, and almost no factories. The Russian Orthodox Church considered it a sin to study anything that was not in the Bible. Change was deemed contrary to God's will, and foreigners were generally regarded as a menace to Russian tradition. There were a few attempts to overcome Russia's isolation from the West, mostly by bringing in European merchants, architects, and army officers. But these attempts had only a limited effect.

Then Peter the Great became the tsar, or ruler, of Russia. By the end of his reign, 1725, he had speeded up the pace of change in his country tremendously and dragged it at least partway into the modern world. In this book, you will learn how he did it and what it cost the Russian people. You will see how the people lived and worked. And you will read poems, plays, legends, and letters in which the Russians themselves tell us about their experiences and beliefs.

Peter the Great helped change Russia's culture, economy, politics, and military power. His subjects called him the Teacher of His People.

The Tsar Wh

PART ONE

Peter towered over most Russians. He was extremely energetic and required only a few hours of sleep each night.

Peter was probably the most inquisitive individual in Russia. He was always trying to figure out how mechanical objects worked. When he was twelve, he learned how to operate a lathe and became an excellent turner in wood and ivory. He ordered a carpenter's bench and was soon working away with hammer, chisel, and ax. Over the next few years, he learned how to shape red-hot iron at the blacksmith's forge and how to set printing type and bind books. He studied arithmetic and trigonometry so he could understand the astrolabe, a navigational device.

Peter's most important discovery took place when he was sixteen. He and a Dutch companion named Franz Timmermann were exploring one of the royal estates when they came upon a locked storehouse. Peter ordered its doors opened and began poking around inside. In a corner lay a half-decayed boat turned upside down. Peter stared at the strange craft. Instead of having a flat bottom like Russian boats, this one had a heavy keel. It also had a pointed bow. "It's an English boat," Timmermann explained. Then he added that with a new mast and sails, it could go against the wind.

The young tsar was astonished. Russian seagoing ships were able to run only *before* the wind. A vessel that could sail *against* the wind opened up all sorts of exciting possibilities!

Peter enjoyed carpentry so much that he later helped build a ship for his navy.

As quickly as possible, Peter had the English boat repaired and learned how to tack against the wind. Then he went out sailing every day. It was the start of the two main interests of his life. One was a love of the sea and a desire to obtain seaports for his almost landlocked nation. The other was a determination to bring western Europe's modern technology and ways of life to Russia.

Early Life

Peter's father, Tsar Alexei Mikhailovich, demanded so much money and manpower from his subjects that, in the late 1600s, Russia's first great peasant uprising broke out.

Peter was born on May 30, 1672, the first son of his father's second wife, Natalya Naryshkina. When he was four years old, his father, the tsar of Russia, died. But Peter did not inherit the throne. It went instead to his half brother Fedor, son of the late tsar's first wife. Six years later, the sickly Fedor likewise died, and this time Peter was named tsar.

But his hold on the title was brief. In addition to Fedor, his late father's first wife had borne another son, Ivan. In contrast to Peter, who was robust and energetic, Ivan was feebleminded, epileptic, and half-blind. However, he was supported by his sister Sofia, who hoped to become regent if her brother were named tsar. (A regent is the person who governs during the period when the rightful ruler is too young to take command.)

A decisive individual, Sofia prepared a plot. With the help of her relatives, the Miloslavskiis, she sent secret agents among the *streltsy* (the musketeers who guarded Moscow, the nation's capital). The agents hinted that the Naryshkins, the family of Peter's mother, had poisoned Fedor and were planning to give foreigners all the top posts in the government and the army. Worse, they were planning to attack the Russian Orthodox Church. Finally, in mid-May 1682, a rumor spread that the Naryshkins had actually strangled Ivan.

The enraged *streltsy* seized their pikes and muskets and marched on the palace. For three days, they stormed through its halls, killing all the Naryshkins they could find. When the bloodshed was over, Ivan and Peter were named joint tsars—with Ivan the senior—under the regency of Sofia. For the next seven years, she

The *streltsy* were the elite of Russia's armed forces. In addition to receiving money, food, and clothing from the tsar, they were exempt from taxation and were allowed to engage in trade when they were not fighting. Many *streltsy* became quite wealthy.

was the real ruler of Russia, closely helped by her lover, Prince Vasilii (Basil) Golitsyn.

During his half sister's regency, Peter lived in the village of Preobrazhenskoe, three miles outside Moscow. He went to the capital's government center, the Kremlin, only to take part in ceremonial functions such as religious festivals and receptions for foreign ambassadors. The rest of his time he spent mostly at war games.

Peter rounded up several hundred young sons of both nobles and peasants, dressed them in Western-style uniforms, and drilled them with the help of officers from the so-called German Quarter, or Foreign Quarter. (This was the suburb of Moscow where all foreigners were required to live. Although Germans formed the majority, the suburb also housed Dutchmen, Englishmen, Frenchmen, and Scots, with a few Danes, Italians, and Swedes.) At first Peter's soldiers were armed only with wooden cannons. Later, the young tsar obtained real brass cannons as well as smaller guns from the national armory. When his men were sufficiently trained, Peter organized them into two competing regiments and staged mock battles. He marched them on long expeditions through the countryside. He had them construct forts of timber and earth, and then attack and defend the forts.

During almost seven years of war games, Peter performed the same duties as his men. He dug trenches and stood watch. He shared the men's food and sleeping quarters. Instead of appointing himself a general, he started out as a drummer boy and worked his way up through the ranks. He wanted to learn soldiering thoroughly.

By now Peter was not quite seventeen. In an age when life was short, he was considered a full-grown man. He certainly looked it, for he stood almost six feet eight inches tall. Only an occasional nervous twitch—probably the result of the three days of terror when the *streltsy* had rioted and murdered several of his relatives—marred his handsome round face. In any event, as his mother kept reminding him, it was the duty of a tsar to marry and produce a son. So in 1689 Peter agreed to wed Evdokia Lopukhina, a pretty noblewoman, who was three years older than himself. Unfortunately, Evdokia was timid, dull, uneducated, and suspicious of everything foreign. Although she bore a son, named Alexei (a second son died in infancy), the couple soon became so estranged that they stopped talking to each other.

In the meantime, Sofia's position as regent was deteriorating. Two military campaigns in the Crimea (a peninsula that extends into the Black Sea; at this time, its inhabitants owed allegiance to the Turks) led by Prince Golitsyn had turned into disasters. She had antagonized many nobles when she began calling herself an autocrat, a title normally reserved for tsars. There were rumors that she planned to marry Golitsyn and overthrow Ivan and Peter. When she mobilized the *streltsy*, the tension in Moscow rose even higher.

Matters finally came to a head in mid-August 1689. One of Peter's servants rode into Moscow with a routine dispatch. Several *streltsy* pulled the man from his horse and beat him before dragging him into the palace. Thereupon some *streltsy* who were loyal to Peter sent messengers galloping to Preobrazhenskoe with a warning for the tsar. Aroused from his sleep, Peter leaped from his bed and, in nightgown and bare feet, jumped on a horse and rode into a nearby wood to wait for someone to bring him his clothes. Then he and a group of companions rode forty-five miles to seek refuge in the Trinity Monastery. It was a significant choice for a refuge. Not only was the monastery heavily fortified, it was also a traditional royal sanctuary and one of the holiest places in Russia. The *streltsy* would never attack it.

Nor did they. Instead, each night growing numbers of *streltsy* streamed out of Moscow and came to the monastery to join Peter. So did the Patriarch Joachim, the head of the Russian Orthodox Church. And so too did all the foreign officers of the Russian army.

By mid-September it was clear that Sofia had lost the struggle. Her closest supporters were tortured, executed, or sent into exile. (Prince Golitsyn ended up in Siberia.) Sofia herself was confined to a twelve-room apartment in a convent. There she would spend the remaining fifteen years of her life, visited only by her sisters and aunts and only on holy days. In October 1689, Peter rode, triumphant, into Moscow to the pealing of church bells and the resounding cheers of his subjects.

Sofia was heavy in build, very plain-faced, and intellectually brilliant. By her midteens, she was determined to break out of the dull, isolated way of life of Russian noble-women. She ended her days, however, as a nun.

Banquets and Battles

Although Sofia was gone, the young tsar did not take over the reins of government. Instead, he left matters of state to the Naryshkins and matters of ceremony to his half brother Ivan, who was too sickly to do much else. For the next five years, Peter devoted himself to having fun. He struck up a close friendship with a Swiss adventurer named Franz Lefort, and the two men occupied themselves with sailing, drinking, dancing, setting off fireworks, holding archery matches, playing practical jokes, and otherwise amusing themselves. They were joined in these activities by anywhere from eighty to two hundred companions, who were known as the Jolly Company.

Many members of the Jolly Company were foreigners, for Peter was fascinated by the world of the German Quarter. The houses there had stuccoed ceilings rather than exposed beams, and the yards were free from garbage and slops. Flowers grew in window boxes. The men wore tailored coats, knee breeches, and stockings rather than long caftans. Their faces were clean-shaven. They smoked long-stemmed pipes of tobacco and talked about science, trade, and manufacture. Even the women were different. Instead of being shut away in their homes as Russian noblewomen were, the foreign women ate and drank with the men and took part in their conversation. That, Peter decided, was how Russia ought to be.

Peter wanted his country to imitate western Europe in other ways as well. English and Dutch merchants had begun to gain a foothold in Russia. The Europeans hoped to tap the country's natural resources, especially its grain, gold, timber, furs, and hemp. They also hoped to develop overland trade to places such as Persia and China. Peter did not want Russia to become an economic colony of the West. But to prevent that, Russia needed modern Western technology, especially weapons.

Despite his carousing, Peter continued to train his soldiers and to go sailing. In the summer of 1693, he visited Russia's only seaport, Arkhangelsk (Archangel), on the White Sea. Because Arkhangelsk lies just 130 miles south of the Arctic Ocean, its harbor is frozen for six months of the year. During the summer, however, as many as one hundred foreign vessels at a time unloaded and loaded cargo there. Peter had never seen such huge ships before. It was also his first view of the open sea. He became so excited that he promptly began construction of a yacht in which he hoped to explore the Siberian coast in search of a water route to China.

Then, in February 1694, Peter's attitude changed. His mother, Natalya, died at the age of forty-two. The young tsar was desolate, and for the first time he began to think seriously about his government responsibilities. He returned to Arkhangelsk in the spring for some more ocean sailing, and in the early fall he staged his largest war games ever. His thoughts, though, were no longer on mock battles but on real ones.

For more than two centuries, the Turkish-supported Tatars in the Crimea had been raiding villages in southern Russia and capturing hundreds of thousands of Russians to be sold as slaves. The Russian government had launched two campaigns against the Tatars during Sofia's regency, but without success. Now Peter decided that the time had come to secure his country's southern border. He also wanted a second seaport for Russia, a warm-water port that would be open to commerce year-round.

Peter's goal was the fortress town of Azov. Because Azov is situated near the northern tip of the Sea of Azov, its capture would enable Russia to gain access to the Black Sea. From there, Russian ships could move into the Mediterranean Sea and trade directly with western Europe.

The first siege of Azov, in the summer of 1695, was filled with errors on Russia's part. Command was split among three generals, who disagreed about siege tactics, and supply lines often broke down. Furthermore, because the Russians had no oceangoing ships, they were unable to prevent the Turks from provisioning Azov by sea. After fourteen weeks of bitter fighting, Peter ordered a retreat.

Over the winter, the tsar corrected his mistakes. He appointed a single commander for his army and doubled its size. He supervised construction of several seagoing vessels. And he imported Dutch shipwrights and Austrian siege engineers to help when he renewed his campaign in the spring.

This time, Peter was successful. Azov surrendered in July 1696.

The Great Embassy

No sooner had Peter won victory at Azov then he plunged into a series of revolutionary acts. (By now he was the sole tsar, his half brother Ivan having died several months earlier.) First, he ordered construction of Russia's first real naval base. Next, he ordered construction of a full-size navy within eighteen months. Then he sent the sons of more than fifty noble families to Venice, Holland, and England—the world's leading maritime powers—to study seamanship, navigation, and shipbuilding. The young men could not return to Russia without a certificate of skill signed by a foreign master.

Finally, the tsar announced his most dramatic act. He himself would go abroad and spend the next year and a half touring western Europe. He planned to study shipbuilding, recruit technical experts, seek diplomatic allies for a new campaign against the Turks, and in general demonstrate that Russia was now a major power to be reckoned with.

The Great Embassy, as it was called, left Moscow in March 1697. It numbered more than 250 people. To everyone's astonishment, the tsar traveled in disguise. He called himself Bombardier Peter Mikhailov. Of course he could not disguise his height. But he threatened members of the embassy with death if they addressed him by his real title in public.

Peter's first stops—in Sweden and in the German states of

One of Peter's favorite disguises was that of a ship's carpenter.

Peter studies shipbuilding in Holland. Because he worked as hard as they did, his fellow workers at the Dutch shipyard called him Master Peter.

Brandenburg and Hanover—were brief. Then came Holland, where the tsar spent the winter working as a carpenter in a Dutch shipyard. He also visited every place of interest he could: factories, museums, sawmills and paper mills, medical laboratories, botanical gardens, and printing shops. He learned how to cobble shoes, use a microscope, engrave metal, and even how to pull teeth. More importantly, he learned that Holland was rich because it had an educated population and a large commercial fleet. As yet Russia had neither. But it would, if Peter had his way.

After five months in Holland, the tsar continued on to England, where he stayed four months. Again, he inspected factories, workshops, and botanical gardens. He learned still more trades, including that of watchmaker. He observed a sham naval battle by the royal fleet and paid repeated visits to the mint. In those days, there was considerable clipping of coins by thieves. That is, bits of silver or gold were cut from the edges of coins, thus lessening both their weight and their value. England had recently made clipping easy to detect by milling, or making a ridge around a coin's edge. Peter carefully studied the new technique.

The tsar also hired hundreds of experts—doctors, chemists, shipwrights, engineers, navigators, and even barbers—and gave them long-term contracts to work in Russia. He purchased a variety of items to take home, including dental equipment and a coffin built of planks to replace the typical Russian coffin, which was hollowed out from a single block of wood.

At last Peter headed back to Russia. He had not succeeded in obtaining allies for a war against Turkey. But he *had* learned a great deal about modern technology and ways of life. And he was going to teach this to his people—whether they liked it or not.

Early Reforms

Peter started with a show of force. During his absence, some 2,000 *streltsy* had revolted. Although the revolt had been easily suppressed, Peter was convinced that it was part of a plot to restore Sofia to the throne. Accordingly, the tsar had fourteen torture chambers constructed at Preobrazhenskoe, and for weeks, they were filled with the screams and moans of men being beaten or roasted over open flames. Although no tangible evidence of a plot was uncovered, Peter decided to get rid of the *streltsy* as a possible threat to his power. He had more than 1,000 of them executed, either by hanging, beheading, or being broken on the wheel. Then he disbanded the remaining 16,000, confiscated their houses and their weapons, and exiled them, together with their families, to Siberia and other distant parts of Russia.

Now reform began in earnest. First, Peter attacked what he considered to be his people's backward appearance. He ordered men to cut off their beards. This shocked the Orthodox Russians. Had not God made man in His image? they asked. Was not Jesus bearded? It was blasphemous to shave! they cried. But Peter insisted, and soon everyone at the court, in government service, or in the army was clean-shaven. (Many, however, carefully put their beards aside to be buried with them when they died.) Merchants and peasants were allowed to keep their beards upon payment of a beard tax. Only priests and monks were exempt from the rule.

Peter often carried a pair of shears around with him in order to cut off men's beards.

Peter then ordered people to adopt new clothing styles. No more long caftans with wide, dangling sleeves for men; no more shoes with turned-up toes. They were impractical for marching in the army or working in a shipyard. Instead, men were to wear Western-style short coats, breeches, and boots. Noblewomen were to leave off their bulky overdresses and limit themselves to petticoats and skirts. Moreover, noblewomen were no longer to be kept secluded, or shut away in their homes. They were to be invited to weddings and other public entertainments, and they were to sit in the same room with the men.

Peter's first reforms were symbolic more than anything else. His next changes were fundamental.

One change had to do with the calendar. Russians numbered

the years beginning with the supposed creation of the world. The calendar used in western Europe, however, based dates on the birth of Christ. Thus, the Great Embassy had returned to Moscow in 7206, according to the Russian calendar, not in 1698. Peter insisted that Russia adopt the Western calendar.

Other changes had to do with education. The tsar adapted the Cyrillic alphabet used by the Russians to movable type and sponsored the printing of books on topics ranging from geometry to etiquette. (Until that time, almost all books printed in Russia had been religious texts.) Peter is even said to have edited a few of the books himself, mostly by crossing out unnecessary words. He replaced the existing Slavic numerals with easier-to-use Arabic numbers. He established several elementary schools, two medical schools, a scientific and technical school, a public library, and a museum. He also ordered the sons of nobles to study abroad for five years and did not permit them to marry until they had mastered reading, writing, arithmetic, geometry, and the study of fortifications.

Russian		Roman Equivalent	Approximate Sound in English
А	а	a	*far*
Б	б	b	*bog*
В	в	v	*vault*
Г	г	g	*go*
Д	д	d	*dog*
Е	е	ye	*yet*
Ё	ё	yo	*yawl*
Ж	ж	zh	*azure*
З	з	z	*zone*
И	и	i	*feet*
Й	й	y	*boy*
К	к	k	*kid*
Л	л	l	*law*
М	м	m	*moose*
Н	н	n	*not*
О	о	o	*awe*

The Cyrillic alphabet has thirty-three letters. Here are examples of the way some of the letters are written and their approximate sounds in English.

The Great
Northern War

Peter wanted goods, ideas, technology, and skilled people to flow
into Russia from western Europe. But Turkey blocked Russia's
access to the Black Sea and Sweden blocked its access to the Baltic
Sea. To Peter, the only way to remove these obstacles was war.
And in fact, warfare was constant throughout his reign.

After Peter failed to obtain European allies for a campaign
against the Turks to the south, he shifted his attention northward.
Sweden, however, was a formidable opponent. Not only did it
control most of the territory around the Baltic, but it also had
what was probably the best army in Europe.

The struggle began in 1700. The Russians opened by attacking
the Swedish town of Narva. But their gunpowder was unreliable
and their cannons misfired. Moreover, they soon ran out of ammu-
nition. A surprise counterattack by the Swedes, combined with a
blinding snowstorm, led to a resounding defeat for Peter's army.

The tsar was not discouraged, however. As he had after his
defeat at Azov, he began to correct his mistakes. To insure a steady
supply of troops, he ordered that peasants be drafted into the
army for life. To improve the caliber of officers, he insisted that
soldiers be promoted on the basis of ability and length of service,
not family background. To improve the army's striking power, he

In 1710 Russia did not have a single warship on the Baltic Sea. By 1725 it had 48 warships, as well as 750 smaller vessels.

introduced the use of the flintlock and the bayonet. To supply his army, he had new iron mines opened and new factories set up to produce guns, uniforms, ships, and sails. Working conditions in the mines and factories were extremely harsh. But Russia gradually became industrialized.

In 1704 Peter avenged his humiliation at Narva by capturing the town. His greatest victory, however, took place in 1709.

The Swedes had invaded Russia the previous year and were attempting to advance on Moscow. To delay the enemy, the Russians adopted a scorched-earth policy. That is, they burned their own countryside to prevent the Swedes from obtaining food and other supplies. The Swedish army was further damaged by one of the coldest winters in European history. It was so cold that wine froze in people's cellars and squirrels fell dead from the trees. Thousands of Swedish soldiers either died of exposure or lost their ears, noses, fingers, or toes due to frostbite.

In mid-June 1709, Peter took personal command of his army, saying, "Soldiers: the hour has struck when the fate of the whole motherland lies in your hands. Either Russia will perish or she will be reborn in a nobler shape. . . . Of Peter it should be known that he does not value his own life, but only that Russia should live in piety, glory and prosperity." Two weeks later, the Russians destroyed the Swedish army at the battle of Poltava.

Despite this great victory, the war dragged on for another twelve years. During that time, Peter was forced to return Azov to the Turks, who had allied themselves with Sweden. On the other hand, he built a Baltic fleet and trained enough seamen to win a naval victory—Russia's first ever—at Hangö in 1714.

Finally, in 1721, Russia and Sweden signed a peace treaty ending the Great Northern War. Russia received the entire Baltic coast from Vyborg in Finland to Riga in what is now Latvia. The tsar was given the title of Peter the Great, Father of Our Country, Emperor of All Russia. Russia was now a major player on the European scene.

More Changes

In order to fight the Great Northern War effectively, Peter not only needed a stronger army and navy. He also needed huge sums of money. As he once wrote, "Money is the lifeblood of war." Accordingly, he imposed a host of new taxes on the Russian people.

Peter replaced the existing household tax with a soul tax, or head tax, on all males except nobles and clergymen. Every man was to be taxed regardless of his age or ability to pay. Even minor children were taxed. This arrangement more than doubled peasants' taxes.

The tsar found other ways to collect money. Formal contracts and documents had to be printed on stamped paper sold by the government. The government also had a monopoly on the sale of salt, tobacco, alcohol, tar, playing cards, chess pieces, furs, and coffins. There was a tax on births, another one on marriages, and still another one on funerals. There were taxes on chimneys and firewood, on beds and bathhouses, on collars for horses and tallow for candles. The tsar even levied a tax on drinking water.

To make certain the people did not protest their financial burdens, Peter set up Russia's first regularly organized secret police. The Secret Office was given authority over all crimes, especially treason "by word or deed." Spies and informers were encouraged to report any sign of discontent, and anyone who was denounced to the Secret Office was tortured and executed.

While Peter was carrying out these public changes, he made some changes in his personal life as well. He forced his wife, Evdokia, to enter a convent, thus in effect divorcing her. Some time later, he fell deeply in love with a young Lithuanian peasant girl named Catherine Skavronskaia. She was not only handsome but also fun-loving, energetic, kind, and extremely good-natured—in short, a perfect companion for the tsar. She often traveled with him on diplomatic journeys and military campaigns. And she bore his children—twelve in all, of whom only two lived past the age of seven. In 1707 Peter married her in secret, and in 1712 he married her again, this time in public. She was crowned tsaritsa in 1724.

After Peter's death, his wife ruled as Empress Catherine I from 1725 to 1727. She died at the age of forty-three.

"Window on the West"

Peter had always disliked Moscow. To him, it symbolized Russia's backward past. It was also a reminder of the frightening three days when he and his relatives had been at the mercy of the rioting *streltsy*. Accordingly, in 1703 he began work on a new city that would be everything Moscow was not.

The site Peter chose for St. Petersburg, named after the tsar's patron saint, lay at the mouth of the Neva River on land lately won from Sweden. It seemed a poor choice. The ground was a swampy wasteland and the air in summer was filled with mosquitoes. When the west wind blew, the Neva, unable to flow into the sea, rose and flooded its banks. Few crops could grow in the area. Drinking water was scarce. The harbor was frozen for six months of the year. And when the ice broke in the spring, it was impossible to travel over the roads.

But all Peter saw was that the site faced the Baltic Sea. That meant St. Petersburg's inhabitants would have direct contact with western Europe. As for construction problems, the Dutch had tamed the sea in building their city of Amsterdam. So why couldn't the Russians do the same?

Gradually, St. Petersburg began to take shape. Lumber came from inland forests; bricks and tiles were manufactured in new local factories. The main problem was stone: none was available in the vicinity. So Peter ordered every carriage, cart, and ship that entered the city to bring with it a certain number of stones. He also forbade stonemasons to work anywhere else in Russia but St. Petersburg.

Construction was directed by architects imported from western Europe, especially Italy and France. Forced labor provided the manpower. The working conditions were frightful. Lodgings were filthy. Food was in short supply. The drafted peasants lacked wheelbarrows and had to carry earth in their clothing. They often worked in water up to their waists. Accidents and diseases such as dysentery, malaria, and scurvy were common. It is estimated that from 30,000 to 100,000 people died building St. Petersburg. It was truly "a city built on bones."

It was also an expensive city, since most food and other provisions had to be imported from farther south. Between the high cost of living, the frequent floods and fires, and occasional attacks by wolves from the nearby forests, no one wanted to live there. But Peter was not to be thwarted. He simply ordered people to move there from Moscow. By 1714 St. Petersburg—now the country's new capital—had about 35,000 inhabitants. By 1724 the figure had doubled.

By then too the city was on its way to becoming a beautiful place. The new buildings along the canals and the Neva River were generally made of stone, while the city's older buildings, which were made of wood, were gradually being replaced by stone structures. (The only exceptions were the shacks of the poor, which were made of logs.) Fountains sparkled in the garden of the tsar's Summer Palace, and a wide stone-paved boulevard called Nevskii Prospekt ran at an angle to the Neva's south bank. Although most other streets were unpaved, they were lined by maple trees. The main squares and thoroughfares were lit at night by lamps. A regular rubbish collection service had been set up, and pigs, cows, and other livestock were not supposed to wander around unless they were accompanied by herdsmen. To improve the city's culture, Peter established several museums, an art gallery, a library, and a zoo. St. Petersburg was unquestionably one of his greatest accomplishments, in spite of its tremendous cost in human lives.

The buildings on Nevskii Prospekt, like others in St. Petersburg, were modeled on designs Peter had admired in western Europe.

The Last Years

A major concern for all rulers is the heir to the throne. In Peter's case, the problem was that he and his son Alexei were opposites in everything except a liking for liquor. Peter was physically strong and personally aggressive; Alexei was sickly and timid. Peter loved war; Alexei was uninterested in military or naval matters. Peter read books on science; Alexei read books on the lives of the saints. Peter wanted to modernize Russia as rapidly as possible; Alexei wanted the country to return to its old-fashioned ways.

In 1711 Alexei married Germany's Princess Charlotte. The marriage was a disaster. Alexei either abused or ignored his wife, and even installed his latest mistress—a Finnish peasant named Afrosina—in the palace. Four years later, Charlotte died after giving birth to her second child. When Alexei returned home after the funeral, he found a letter from his father threatening to disinherit him unless he changed his ways: "I will deprive you of the succession, as one may cut off a useless member [part of the body]. Do not fancy that . . . I only write this to terrify you. . . . I do not spare my own life for my country and . . . my people, why should I spare you? . . . I would rather choose . . . a worthy stranger than . . . my own unworthy son."

The threat of disinheritance did not work. First, Alexei offered to give up the throne and retire to a country estate with Afrosina. Then he offered to become a monk. Finally, he fled to Austria, where he remained in hiding for more than a year until Peter's spies found him. He then agreed to return to Russia if he could marry Afrosina. But when he returned home, instead of marriage he found a father convinced that his son was at the head of a conspiracy to dethrone him. Peter's belief was strengthened when Afrosina betrayed Alexei by telling Peter that his son planned to abandon St. Petersburg and dismantle the navy when he became tsar.

Afraid that all he had accomplished for Russia would be destroyed, Peter disinherited Alexei. He then had his son tortured and put on trial for treason. The court sentenced the prince to death. But before the sentence could be carried out, Alexei died in prison. The official report said the cause of death was a stroke. However, most historians believe he died as a result of having been tortured, while a few historians believe that Peter had him executed in secret.

From then on, Peter worked harder than ever to modernize Russia. He set up more factories and gave loans and tax breaks to the men who ran them. He had a canal built to link the Neva and Volga Rivers, thus enabling goods to move by water between the country's interior and the Baltic Sea. He promoted the timber and mining industries in Siberia. He tried to increase agricultural productivity by ordering farmers to harvest grain with scythes instead of less efficient sickles. He commissioned Danish explorer Vitus Bering to find out if Siberia and North America were connected by land. He tried to stamp out corruption among government officials. And he established the Table of Ranks, which allowed any man in the civil service or the military to work his way up to the nobility "through meritorious service to the state."

Peter also changed the administration of the Russian Orthodox

Alexei (*left*) was probably terrified of his father all his life. After his death, he was buried in the royal vault next to his neglected wife, Charlotte.

Church. He abolished the office of its leader, the patriarch, and replaced it with a synod, or group of church officials. Above the synod was an official appointed by the tsar. In effect, this made the Church a department of the government and helped to weaken its resistance to westernization. Peter also set up an office to prevent monks and monasteries from accumulating too much wealth.

In the summer of 1724, Peter underwent surgery on his

bladder. The moment he felt better, however, he ignored the advice of his doctors to take things easy and resumed his usual frantic pace. In November, while out sailing, he saw a ship in danger of capsizing. He jumped into the icy water and spent several hours helping to rescue the ship's passengers. He developed a fever, followed by a severe intestinal infection. In January the tsar took to his bed. On January 27, 1725, he asked for a writing tablet and managed to write, "Give all to . . ." before becoming delirious. He died the following morning at the age of fifty-two.

Evaluating Peter

In many ways, Peter the Great was a typical despot. He tolerated no opposition. He was brutal in his methods, so brutal, in fact, that hundreds of thousands of Russians fled abroad to escape the draft, forced labor, and the heavy tax burden. To the tsar, the Russian people were not individuals so much as they were tools with which to accomplish what he wanted.

Yet what Peter wanted above all else was the good of Russia. He wanted it to be part of the modern world. He wanted it to be a strong, prosperous, and educated nation. With unbounded energy and determination, he tried to achieve in one generation what had taken the nations of western Europe several hundred years.

Some of Peter's administrative reforms fell by the wayside after his death. The peasantry did not become westernized until the 1900s. Nevertheless, the Russia that Peter left behind was a very different country from what it had been when he mounted the throne. It was more enlightened, more open to new ideas, more industrialized, and much more powerful.

Probably Russia would have become westernized in any event. But it was Peter the Great who dramatized the need for change and who propelled his country forward on its new path.

PART TWO

Russians have always loved their land despite its difficult climate. In Peter's time, they often referred to it as Holy Mother Russia.

Even in the time of Peter the Great, Russia was the largest country in the world. It stretched for more than 5,000 miles from the Baltic Sea in the west to the Pacific Ocean in the east. From the Arctic Ocean south, it ran for 1,500 to 2,500 miles.

Most of Russia is an immense plain containing several broad belts of vegetation. In the extreme north is the tundra, a region where the ground is frozen most of the year and only mosses grow in summer. In Peter's day, its sparse population consisted mainly of hunters and fur trappers. South of the tundra is the taiga, a band of thick forests—mostly fir, pine, and birch—that furnishes fuel, lumber for houses and boats, sweet honey, and a home for wolves and bears. Next comes the steppe, a treeless area covered by tall grasses. Although its soil is thick, black, and extremely rich, rainfall here is light. Rainfall is also light in the taiga. As a result, Russian farmers have often had trouble growing enough food to feed all the people.

Russia's climate is extremely harsh. Icy winds and blizzards begin sweeping down from the north in early autumn. By late autumn, the land is blanketed in snow, while the rivers and most of the coastal harbors are frozen to a depth of three feet or more. Winters are long and bitterly cold, with little sunlight to brighten the days. The sudden spring thaw brings floods, as rivers overflow

A Russian village in the steppe

their banks with melting ice and snow.

The steppe has played an important role throughout Russia's long history. Since this treeless plain could be easily crossed, it helped tie the Russian people together. Language, religion, and culture spread quickly. At the same time, however, the steppe provided invaders with easy access. From 700 B.C.E.* to the time of Peter the Great, eight waves of nomadic tribes from central Asia poured into Russia. One of these tribes, the Mongols, occupied most of the country between 1237 and 1480 C.E. There were numerous invasions from nations to the west as well, notably Sweden in 1240, Lithuania and Poland in the mid-1300s, Poland again in the mid-1600s, France in 1812, and Germany during World War I (1914–1918) and again during World War II (1939–1945).

*Many systems of dating have been used by different cultures throughout history. This series of books uses B.C.E. (Before Common Era) and C.E. (Common Era) instead of B.C. (Before Christ) and A.D. (Anno Domini) out of respect for the diversity of the world's peoples.

ATLANTIC

OCEAN

SWEDEN

WHITE
SEA

Arkangelsk

Vyborg

Hangö

Neva River

St. Petersburg

Narva

RUSSIA

NORTH
SEA

BALTIC SEA

Riga

DENMARK

Trinity Monastery

Moscow

Moskva River

Preobrazhenskoe

URAL MOUNTAINS

ENGLAND

HOLLAND

Amsterdam

POLAND

Kiev

Poltava

AUSTRIA

Dnieper River

Don River

Volga River

Azov

SEA
OF AZOV

ARAL SEA

CRIMEA

BLACK SEA

CASPIAN SEA

OTTOMAN EMPIRE

MEDITERRANEAN SEA

AFRICA

PETER THE GREAT'S RUSSIA

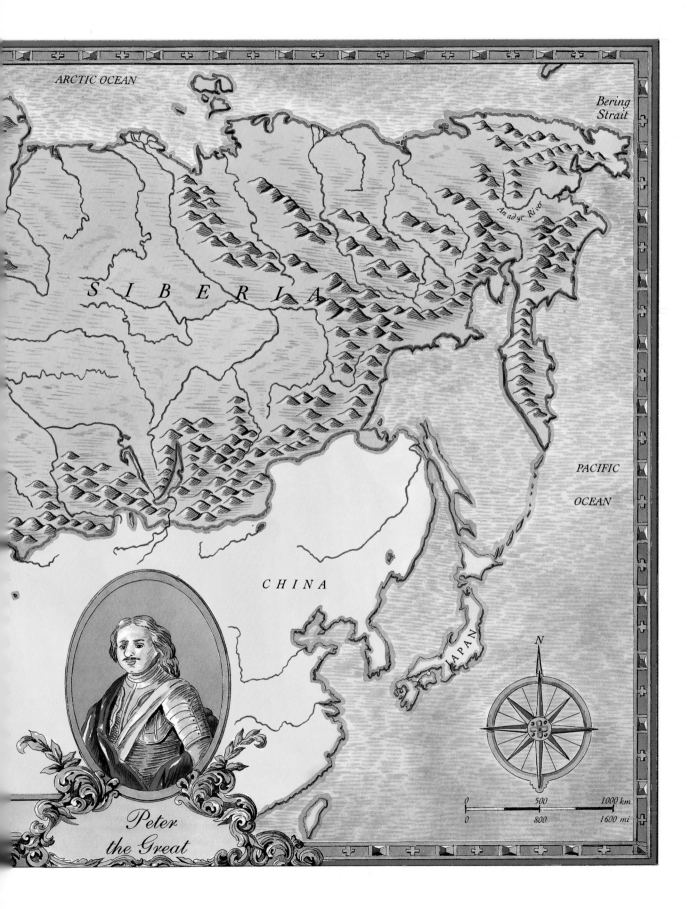

ARCTIC OCEAN

Bering
Strait

Anadyr River

S I B E R I A

PACIFIC

OCEAN

CHINA

JAPAN

N

Peter
the Great

0		500		1000 km
0		800		1600 mi

The Russian Orthodox Church

Peter the Great ruled a people devoted to their church. Nearly all Russians belonged to the Orthodox Church. (The Orthodox Church is the eastern branch of Christianity. In 1054 C.E., the Christian world had split into the Roman Catholic Church and the Orthodox Church over the issue of whether or not the pope in Rome was Christianity's rightful spiritual leader.)

The Russian people attended services faithfully. They observed all the required fasts. They devoted one out of three days of the year to religious holidays. They filled the land with churches and monasteries. They named their children after various saints—and the children celebrated the saints' feast days instead of their own birthdays. Every trade had its patron saint, who was thought to bring good fortune to its members. All Russians had a personal guardian saint or angel to whom they prayed and who were believed to protect them in times of danger.

The Russians called their churches "palaces of God." Interior walls and ceilings were covered with gold, silver, and sacred images known as icons. There were icons of Jesus Christ, the Virgin Mary—or, as the Russians liked to call her, the "Mother of God"—and saints and angels. Some icons consisted of wooden panels painted in vivid reds, yellows, blues, and greens, often with

The artists who painted icons like this one were believed to be divinely inspired. Their brushes and paints were formally blessed before being used.

a gold background. Other icons were mosaics, made by setting small colored pieces of marble, stone, or tile in plaster. Dozens of candles cast a soft light in the splendid buildings, while the air was filled with clouds of perfumed smoke.

Churches were built with a certain number of domes, usually either five or thirteen. Each dome was topped by a cross. A five-domed church had a large central dome and four smaller ones around it. The large dome symbolized Jesus Christ. The smaller domes represented the four writers of the Gospels—Matthew, Mark, Luke, and John. A thirteen-domed church stood for Jesus Christ and the Twelve Apostles. Originally the domes were round,

Foreigners were amazed when they first saw the elaborate and colorful domes of the Cathedral of St. Basil the Blessed in Moscow. It was built in the 1500s, during the reign of Tsar Ivan IV, often called Ivan the Terrible. Legend has it that he gouged out the eyes of the cathedral's architects so they would never again create anything so beautiful.

but by the twelfth century they had taken on the shape of an onion bulb and were pointed on top.

Every church boasted a collection of copper and silver bells. They were of different sizes, up to 180 tons, and were rung in various combinations. The bells rang for all sorts of events in addition to church services, including fires, festivals, marriages, and funerals.

Church services varied in length. A Sunday service in the typical parish church generally lasted about two and a half to three hours. A service for Lent in one of Moscow's cathedrals might run for seven hours. Everyone stood, since there were no seats. An impressive part of the service was the procession. This was usually led by a deacon, who carried the gold-covered Book of the Gospels from the altar to the central part of the church and back again while a male choir sang. The Russians did not allow organs or other musical instruments in their services. They believed that since these instruments had neither life nor souls, they could not be used to praise God.

The most joyful religious holiday of the year was Easter, which the Russians celebrated for fourteen days. During this time, everyone carried hard-boiled colored eggs around with them. When they met someone they knew, they would give the person an egg, kiss him or her once on each cheek, and say, "Christ has risen," to which the other person would reply, "Truly he has risen."

Another religious holiday was devoted to blessing the nation's rivers. In Moscow a mile-long procession made its way through the city streets to the Moskva River. First came two deacons carrying banners, one showing the Mother of God, the other showing Saint Michael fighting a dragon. Then came various church officials, walking two by two. They were followed by the tsar and all his nobles. When the procession reached the river, a great hole was cut in the ice. The highest-ranking church official recited prayers calling on the devil to come out of the water. He then threw frankincense (a sweet-smelling tree gum) down the hole to make the water holy. That was the signal for people to fill their pails with water to take home to drink. Some people even dipped their children's heads into the river, while others jumped in themselves.

Food and Drink

In addition to going to church and celebrating religious holidays, Russians spent considerable time eating and drinking. Unfortunately, their diet was limited. Fresh fruit, green vegetables, and meat were just about unheard-of, although chicken and salted fish were served on some occasions. Most people lived mainly on rye bread, cabbages, and cucumbers, with the addition of beets, carrots, garlic, and onions. The beets were often made into a soup called borscht. It was served either hot or cold, with a spoonful of sour cream to improve its taste.

The nobility, in contrast, ate lavishly. On festival days, the tsar's table held as many as seventy different dishes. A feast began with hors d'oeuvres: pickled mushrooms, eggplant ratatouille, cold sausages, and dumplings stuffed with meat, eggs, fish, cabbage, or rice. Then came soups, followed by heavily seasoned roasts of beef, mutton, and pork. Fish dishes such as salmon and sturgeon were often added. Desserts included cakes, cheeses, fruits, and preserves.

The Russians drank a sort of beer called kvass, as well as mead, a wine made from various fruits. They also drank a great deal of vodka, a colorless, tasteless, but very strong alcoholic drink made from fermented grain.

As a matter of fact, drinking was probably the chief pleasure of the Russian people, especially the men. Every village had a tavern where the men gathered in the evenings and on holidays, sang sad songs, and drank as much as they could afford to buy. A popular saying ran, "The church is near but the road is icy; the tavern is far, but I will walk very carefully." Guests at dinner parties given by nobles were expected to drink enough to put them under the table, at which point they would be carried home. People often dropped down dead drunk in the streets. Even priests and monks consumed huge amounts of liquor.

There were occasional attempts to combat drinking, but they always ran into snags. That was because the government obtained a large part of its revenue from the sale of vodka.

Village taverns were always crowded.

Having Fun

The Russians enjoyed themselves in many other ways besides drinking. They liked to have fun, even though the Russian Orthodox Church frowned on dancing, singing, storytelling, and games.

A favorite winter sport for nobles and peasants alike was sledding. People would build artificial wooden hills, as high as thirty-five feet, with steps on one side and a slope on the other. Then they would pour water on the slope, wait for it to freeze, and slide down on two-passenger sleds.

In early spring, before the arrival of the solemn season of Lent, Russians let off steam with a week-long carnival. There were swings and rides in the central square of every town and village, and dancing in the streets. Troupes of traveling actors performed plays, while acrobats and jugglers showed off their skills. There were open-air fistfights and wrestling matches, as well as bloody contests between a bear and dogs or even between a bear and a man. Sometimes the bears were trained to dance on their hind legs rather than fight.

Russian nobles amused themselves with more sophisticated sports. These included bear hunting, archery, and races on horseback.

Peasant Life

The vast majority of the Russian people were peasants. They lived in one-room huts called *izby*. In the northern part of the country, *izby* were made of logs insulated with moss. In the southern part of the country, they were made of clay and mud.

An *izba* contained little furniture, usually just a table, a few benches, some earthen pots, and three or four clay or wooden dishes. There were no beds. In summer people slept on the benches. In winter they slept on top of a baked clay stove that took up about one-quarter of the *izba*. Because few *izby* had chimneys, smoke could escape only through the wooden shutters that covered the windows or through a hole in the roof. As a result, the inside of most *izby* was black with soot.

Each *izba* had a "beautiful corner" that contained the family icons. These often pictured Saint Nicholas or the biblical prophet Elijah. Guests entering an *izba* would bow before the icons and cross themselves before joining in the conversation. Families passed down their icons from generation to generation. *Izby* in the northern part of the country also had an ax hanging on one wall. The ax served its owner both as a tool for chopping down trees and as a weapon against the wild animals of the forest.

Peasants' clothes were as simple as their houses. In summer the men wore linen trousers, a long linen shirt—usually white or blue—tied at the waist, and a deep-crowned felt hat. The women wore two long dresses, one on top of the other, plus a kerchief on their heads. Shoes were made of bark. Jewelry consisted of a pair of earrings and a cross worn on a string around the neck. In winter both men and women added a sheepskin coat, a furred cap, gloves, and boots made of leather or felt. People made their own clothes.

The peasants washed their clothes in a nearby river. They washed themselves thoroughly every Saturday afternoon in the local bathhouse. There they would stretch out on a bench in a hot room while a neighbor slapped them with bunches of birch twigs.

In this painting, a peasant family appears to be quite comfortable in their *izba*. In reality, however, the homes of Russian peasants lacked many comforts.

When they were hot and red all over, they would rush outdoors and either pour cold water over themselves or, in winter, fling themselves on the ground and roll about in the snow. Then they would go back into the hot bathhouse.

The peasants' year was divided into two distinct periods. From spring until fall, they plowed the fields, planted seeds, and harvested their crops. From fall until spring, they sheltered themselves from the winter cold and celebrated most of the year's religious holidays.

The peasants usually followed a three-field system of farming in

Russian clothing styles did not change much over the centuries.

which they rotated their crops. One field grew spring crops, which were planted in spring and harvested in August. A second field grew winter crops, which were planted in August and harvested the following summer. The third field was left fallow, or unplanted. The next year, the field that had grown spring crops was left fallow. The field that had grown winter crops was planted with spring crops, and the fallow field was planted with winter crops, and so on. The system was not very productive, since one-third of the land was always fallow, but it helped the soil remain fertile.

Wheat was the main crop grown in the south. Farmers in the north grew mostly rye, along with barley and oats. Plows were made of either wood or iron and were usually drawn by horses or oxen. In very poor peasant families, however, women sometimes pulled the plows.

Russian plows were quite primitive, which was one reason why crop yields were low.

Serfdom

About half of Russia's 13 million or so peasants were serfs. They did not own the land they farmed but instead were permanent tenants of a landlord to whom they were tied. The landlord might be a noble, or the Russian Orthodox Church, or a member of the royal family. A landlord had the right to obtain taxes, rent, and labor from his serfs. In addition, he could sell his serfs or give them away, send them to the army for life, or assign them to work in a factory or mine. Serfs were not allowed to travel, even to a neighboring village, without permission. Serfs who ran away from their masters could be reclaimed at any time, and anyone who sheltered a runaway was severely punished, either with a beating or a heavy fine.

The idea behind serfdom was service to the state, which all Russians were expected to provide. Serfs who were drafted into the army or into forced-labor projects served the state directly. So did those who worked in a government-owned factory or mine. Serfs who remained on the land served the state indirectly by paying taxes. In addition, they supported the nobles so that the nobles were able to also serve the state, either as soldiers or as government officials.

A substantial number of peasants, especially in the north, were state peasants rather than serfs. They lived on state-owned land and owed taxes and services to the government but nothing to an individual landlord. Also, because of Siberia's sparse population and the need to encourage settlers, there was no serfdom in that region.

City Life: Moscow

Until Peter the Great built his new capital of St. Petersburg, Russia's most important city was Moscow. It is first mentioned in historical records in 1147. At that time, it was merely an insignificant town on the left bank of the Moskva River. However, it had the benefit of an excellent location at the center of several north-south and east-west trading routes. It also had the benefit of a series of brave and clever princes, who gradually expanded their political control and eventually, in 1480, drove out the Mongols. In addition, the Russian Orthodox Church established its headquarters there. As a result, by the time Peter mounted the throne, Moscow was not only the country's largest city—with about 200,000 inhabitants out of an overall population of about 15 million—but also a center of trade, religion, and art.

The heart of Moscow was the triangle-shaped Kremlin (the word *kremlin* means "fortress"). Built on a hill overlooking the city, it contained the tsar's palace, three magnificent golden-domed cathedrals, a tall bell tower, government offices, military barracks, bakeries, laundries, stables, and the houses of the most important church officials and nobles. Surrounding the Kremlin was a massive brick wall between thirty and sixty-five feet high and between twelve and twenty feet thick. Some nineteen towers studded the wall, allowing people inside to easily observe any enemy activity outside. Defending soldiers shot guns and arrows

Moscow's huge Red Square , painted seventy-five years after Peter's death, is flanked by the Kremlin's towers. St. Basil's Cathedral is in the background. The word for "red" in Russian also means "beautiful."

through narrow openings in the wall. Additional aids to defense included underground passages, water pipes, and storage spaces for food and weapons. The Kremlin was one of the strongest fortresses in the world.

East of the Kremlin lay Red Square, a vast open space that served as the political and commercial center of Moscow. Here the tsar delivered his speeches from a low stone platform. Nearby, criminals were tortured or executed. Much of the square was filled with rows of shops and stalls. Some were made of wood, while others were covered by canvas. Each row sold a different kind of product, from silk, leather, fur, and pottery to vegetables and fruits. Barbers plied their craft in one area. They worked on a thick carpet of felt, formed from hair that had accumulated over the years. Paintings, penny prints, and books were sold in the stalls lining the Bridge of the Saviour. All the bridges that spanned Moscow's rivers and moats were built of wood, and they frequently held stalls.

East of Red Square was the merchants' and artisans' quarter, called Kitai Gorod. Some scholars say the name came from the baskets (known as *kit* or *kita*) that had been filled with earth and used to strengthen the district's protective wall. Other scholars say that Kitai Gorod means "middle city" and refers to the fact that the quarter occupied Moscow's central area.

The merchants engaged in both domestic and international trade. They imported meat from the northern regions of Russia, fish from the southern regions, and furs from Siberia. From Europe they imported mostly weapons and luxury goods, generally in exchange for raw materials such as leather, grain, and furs. Transporting these items, especially domestic ones, was difficult. Whenever it rained or the snow melted, the roads became a sea of mud. As a result, Russian merchants had only two practical options: riverboats in summer and ice sleds in winter.

Kitai Gorod's artisans practiced about 250 different crafts. Icon painting was a flourishing industry. Metalworkers turned out iron gates and window shutters to protect Moscow's inhabitants from burglars. Armorers made helmets, coats of mail, and parade armor. Coppersmiths produced crosses and cooking utensils, while

This scene shows a crossroads in Kitai Gorod. The building to the right is an inn and tavern. The men sitting on the ground in front of it are prisoners begging passersby for food. (Moscow did not feed its prisoners.) The building to the left is the local poorhouse and morgue. In front of it are corpses in coffins waiting to be identified by relatives.

tileworkers created glazed and colored tiles for decorating both churches and heating stoves. Carpenters produced lumber of varying lengths. Moscow's mostly wooden houses frequently burned down. All a buyer had to do was tell a carpenter the size and number of rooms for which he needed lumber. The lengths could be delivered and the new house assembled within a few days.

On the outskirts of the Kremlin, Red Square, and Kitai Gorod was a horseshoe-shaped district known as the White City. It was surrounded by a white stone wall and contained a mixture of churches and the houses of nobles and merchants. The houses were mostly two-storied. On the first floor were storage rooms and the servants' living quarters. The nobles and merchants lived on the second floor. Windows were decorated on the outside with carved and painted ornaments. An exterior stairway contained several big landings where the house's owner welcomed his guests.

Surrounding all four areas of Moscow was an outermost district called the Earthen City. There, in tiny log huts along log-paved streets, lived Moscow's poorest workers. This district also contained several fortress-monasteries.

Life in Moscow followed a regular pattern. Mornings were filled with activity. At noon people ate their main meal and then took a rest for several hours. Traffic ceased, while shopkeepers went to sleep in front of their booths. Activity resumed in midafternoon. At dusk the shops were closed with heavy shutters, and the gates to the main streets were locked. People seldom ventured out after dark.

Life was often unpleasant and dangerous for Moscow's residents. The winding streets were filthy and filled with beggars and drunks. Fires were so common that the government forbade the use of heating stoves in homes and public bathhouses during the summer. There were no streetlights, and nighttime robberies were common. So were nighttime murders. In fact, every morning the police collected the bodies lying in the streets and brought them to the City Yard for identification by relatives or friends.

Personal Matters

Perhaps because they were so fond of drink, Russian men were noted for their coarse and abusive language. They flung blood-curdling oaths at anyone who annoyed them. Even priests swore at one another. Men frequently quarreled on the streets and in the squares of cities and towns. And the quarrels often led to fistfights.

Russian men ruled their families. Wife-beating was common. Women were supposed to keep quiet when men spoke and to always ask their husbands for permission before leaving the house. They were expected to be sweet, gentle, and obedient at all times. According to a popular book of rules for behavior, "a good wife, who loves labor and is silent and meek, becomes her husband's crown."

Marriages were arranged by the fathers of the couple. The wedding ceremony was performed by a priest. During the ceremony, he held a long, slender candle in each hand to signify hope for a happy marriage. After the ceremony, the bride fell at her groom's feet and knocked her head upon his shoe to show that she would obey him. In turn, the groom held part of his shirt over his bride as a sign that he would protect and cherish her. Next, the groom's father gave the bride's father a loaf of bread. The bride's father promised to deliver the agreed-upon dowry. Then he broke the loaf into pieces and distributed them to the members of both families. This showed that the two families were now one.

Unmarried Russian girls wore their hair in two braids that dangled down their backs. After marriage they put their hair up. Children under ten, both girls and boys, wore their hair cut short.

Women who lived in cities wore a great deal of makeup. They had whitened faces with red cheeks and black eyebrows. The story is told that one day a prince's wife decided to leave her makeup off in order to display her natural beauty. But the wives of the prince's friends would have none of it. They complained so bitterly to their husbands that the men went to the prince and told him that he had to make his wife put on makeup like the other women.

When people got sick, there were numerous folk remedies at hand. A favorite was cupping. Small heated glass cups were placed on a person's bare back. As the cups cooled off, the suction puffed the skin into the cup. This supposedly drew away the bad blood that had caused the illness. The cups were removed after ten minutes or so. The red circles they left usually went away after two weeks.

Not surprisingly, remedies like this often failed to cure a seriously ill person. Russians who died in wintertime could not be buried because the ground was frozen too hard for spades or pickaxes to penetrate it. Accordingly, the bodies were kept frozen in a special house until the spring thaw. Then a small scroll was put into the hand of each corpse. The scroll stated that the dead person was a Russian who had lived and died in the Orthodox faith. Russians believed that Saint Peter had to read a person's scroll before he would admit that person into heaven. The corpse was then placed in a coffin and buried to the accompaniment of loud cries and weeping from specially hired women mourners.

The marker over the person's grave showed three names. All

Russians had three names, to explain whose son or daughter they were. For example, Peter the Great was Pyotr Alexeyevich (son of Alexei) Romanov. The author of this book was born Mara Grigorevna (daughter of Grigorii) Baraks. If she had been a Russian noblewoman who had married Peter, she would have become Mara Grigorevna Romanova.

The colors of this woman's makeup are as bright as those of her clothing.

PART THREE

The Russiaı

Several Russian stories and novels contain lyrical descriptions of the beauty of the steppe, especially its wildflowers.

The first Russian state was founded by Oleg. A well-known legend tells how a magician predicted this ruler's death in 912 C.E.:

Thus Oleg ruled . . . and dwelt at peace with all nations.

Now autumn came, and Oleg bethought him of his horse that he had caused to be well fed, yet had never mounted. For on one occasion he had made inquiry of the wonder-working magicians as to the ultimate cause of his death. One magician replied, "O Prince, it is from the steed which you love and on which you ride that you shall meet your death." Oleg then reflected, and determined never to mount this horse or even to look upon it again. So he gave command that the horse should be properly fed, but never led into his presence. He thus let several years pass. . . . He [then] . . . summoned his senior squire and inquired as to the whereabouts of the horse. . . . The squire answered that he was dead. Oleg laughed and mocked the magician, exclaiming, "Soothsayers tell untruths, and their words are naught but falsehood. This horse is dead, but I am still alive."

Then he commanded that a horse should be saddled. "Let me see his bones," said he. He rode to the place where the bare bones and the skull lay. Dismounting from his

horse, he laughed, and remarked, "Am I to receive my
death from this skull?" And he stamped upon the skull with
his foot. But a serpent crawled forth from it and bit him in
the foot, so that in consequence he sickened and died. All
the people mourned for him in great grief. They bore him
away and buried him upon the hill. . . . His tomb stands
there to this day, and it is called the Tomb of Oleg.

In the early 1400s, two monks living in the city of Kiev helped to collect a mass of historical and cultural material that came to be called the *Primary Chronicle*. Among the writings is a story— probably more a legend—that tells how the Russian people converted to Christianity.

Originally the people were pagans. They worshipped many gods and celebrated religious holidays with song, dance, and drink. Around 988 C.E., however, Prince Vladimir I, the ruler of Russia, invited missionaries from different faiths to help him choose a new religion for his people. He rejected Islam because it forbade the drinking of wine, and—as he put it—"drink is the joy of the Russian." He also rejected Judaism because the Jews had failed in their revolt against the Romans in the second century C.E. and had lost Palestine, their homeland. To Vladimir, this meant that the Jewish God had no political power—and that would never do for the Russians. Vladimir then faced a choice between the two branches of Christianity, the one that used Latin in its services and the one that used Greek. To help him make up his mind, he sent out ten envoys to Germany and Greece to observe the different Christian services and report back to him. The *Primary Chronicle* describes the results of their journey:

The envoys reported: . . . "We went among the Germans, and saw them performing many ceremonies in their temples; but we beheld no glory there. Then we went on to Greece, and the Greeks led us to the edifices [buildings] where they worship their God, and we knew not whether we were in heaven or on earth. For on earth there is no such splendor or such beauty, and we are at a loss how to describe it. We know only that God dwells there among men, and their service is fairer than the ceremonies of other nations. For we cannot forget that beauty. Every man, after tasting something sweet, is afterward unwilling to accept that which is bitter." . . .

[So] the people were baptized, [and] Vladimir, rejoicing that he and his subjects now knew God himself, . . . ordained that churches should be built and established where pagan idols had previously stood. . . . He began to found churches and to assign priests through out the cities, and to invite the people to accept baptism in all the cities and towns. . . . Vladimir was enlightened . . . and his country with him.

During the twelfth and thirteenth centuries, Russia was invaded by various nomadic tribes from central Asia. In 1185 Russian forces led by Prince Igor suffered a major disaster at the hands of the Kumans. The disaster is described in an epic poem called *The Lay of Igor's Campaign*. It was apparently written by a follower of Prince Igor who probably took part in his master's unsuccessful struggle:

Igor spoke to his warriors:

"Brethren and warriors!
It is better to be killed in battle,
than to become a captive.
Let us mount our swift steeds, brethren!
Let us view the blue river Don.
. . . .

I want to break a lance at the Kuman frontier.
I want, oh, my Russians,
either to drink with you Don [water] from my
 helmet,
or to leave my head there."
. . . .

This battle scene, which was painted by an unknown artist
around 1460, is believed to be the first picture in Russian art
that shows action. Note the angel assisting the army on the
left, which of course was victorious.

Igor awaits his dear brother, Vesvolod [who comes to him and] speaks:

"Brother, . . . my [swift steeds] are ready.

. . . .

My men of Kursk are famed as warriors.
They were swaddled under trumpets.
They were brought up under helmets.
They were fed at lance point.
The roads are known to them.
The ravines are familiar to them.
Their bows are taut,
their quivers are open,
their sabers have been sharpened.
They race into the prairie like gray wolves,
seeking honor for themselves
and glory for their prince."
Then Prince Igor set his foot in the golden stirrup
and rode into the open prairie.

. . . .

[Sometime later the battle began.]

From early morning to night,
from evening to dawn
there flew tempered arrows,
swords rained down upon helmets.

. . . .

The black earth under the hooves
was strewn with bones,
was covered with blood.

. . . .

They fought for one day.

They fought for another day.
At noon on the third day Igor's banners fell.

. . . .

The grass withered from sorrow,
and the saddened trees drooped earthward.

. . . .

Prince Igor exchanged his golden saddle of a prince
for the saddle of a slave.
And the cities became saddened
and joy vanished.

The *Domostroi* is a collection of rules for everyday life, aimed mainly at the nobles and merchants. It probably dates from the mid-1500s:

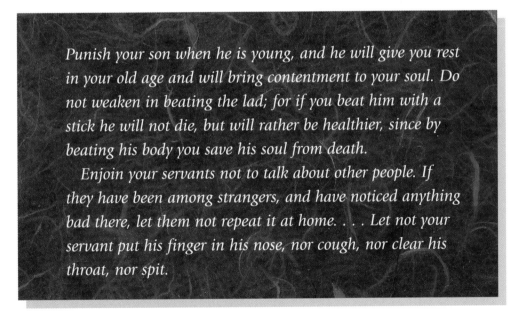

Punish your son when he is young, and he will give you rest in your old age and will bring contentment to your soul. Do not weaken in beating the lad; for if you beat him with a stick he will not die, but will rather be healthier, since by beating his body you save his soul from death.

Enjoin your servants not to talk about other people. If they have been among strangers, and have noticed anything bad there, let them not repeat it at home. . . . Let not your servant put his finger in his nose, nor cough, nor clear his throat, nor spit.

The Russians added popular sayings to the rules of the *Domostroi*. The sayings were well suited to an agricultural economy, since they usually involved animals:

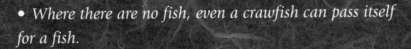

- *Where there are no fish, even a crawfish can pass itself for a fish.*
- *If you're a rooster, crow; if you're a hen, lay eggs.*
- *A cow may be black, but it gives white milk.*
- *You can pull and pull, but you can't milk a bull.*
- *Act like a sheep if you want to bring a wolf.*
- *Lie down with dogs and you'll get up with fleas.*

In the 1600s, Prince Ivan M. Katyrev-Rostovsky wrote *The Book of Annals*, an account of people and events during the sixteenth and early seventeenth centuries. Following are his descriptions of some tsars of the period:

Tsar Ivan IV, the Awesome, often called the Terrible, who reigned from 1533 to 1584:

> *Tsar Ivan was physically unattractive, had gray eyes, a hooked and long nose, and was tall, lean, and with broad shoulders and chest. He had great physical prowess and was . . . well-read, erudite, and very eloquent. He was fearsome to the enemy, and was always prepared to fight for the fatherland. He was cruel to his subjects, . . . being always ready to spill their blood, and both merciless and daring at killing. He ordered that many people be slain, from infants to the aged; he laid waste to many of his own cities; and many clergymen were thrown into prison and mercilessly executed at his orders.*

. . . This Tsar Ivan did many good things, however, and he cared very much for his armies, generously rewarding them from his treasury.

Tsar Boris Godunov, who reigned from 1598 to 1605:

Tsar Boris shone in the full bloom of his handsome appearance. . . . He was of average stature. He was a man of great intelligence, had a marvelous power of reasoning, and was . . . [an] eloquent orator. He was a faithful Christian, gave generously to the poor, and was a great builder. He spent much time on state affairs and he performed a great many marvelous deeds. He had, however, two great shortcomings. . . : he used to go too much to doctors, and he . . . dared to slay those who should have been tsars before himself. And for such deeds he received divine retribution [punishment].

Ivan IV was mentally unbalanced; all his life, he alternated between good and bad periods. On the one hand, he liberalized Russia's law code. On the other hand, while in a terrible rage, he killed his elder son by striking the youth with a heavy staff.

Tsar Vasily Shuisky, who reigned from 1606 to 1610:

Tsar Vasily was short of stature, physically very unattractive, and had eyes that were dull, as if he were blind. He was rather cultured, and his reasoning was sound and pointed. He cared only for those people who brought him gossip and

rumors about people, and he used to receive such persons with
a joyful face, and with sweet pleasure, did he listen to them.
He was given to sorcery [witchcraft], and cared little for the
military.

In the 1500s Russians began moving eastward into Siberia, mostly in search of furs. They traveled by river and portaged, or carried their boats, from one stream to the next. By 1640 they had reached the Pacific Ocean. The exploration of Siberia—a vast region about four thousand miles wide and two thousand miles long—was filled with all sorts of hardships. The following letter, sent in 1662 to the tsar by explorer Senka (Semon) Dezhnev, deals with some of the difficulties he personally faced:

> *I, your humble servant . . . established a wintering place*
> *and a fort, captured some hostages, and collected . . . as*
> *tribute for your Majesty . . . 234 sables . . . and about*
> *573 pounds of walrus tusk. . . . I too, your humble*
> *servant, with my comrades on the Anandyr [Anadyr]*
> *River humbly gave your Majesty 2 walrus tusks weighing*
> *32 pounds. And tribute from that new Anandyr River is*
> *continuing to come to your Majesty to this day. And I,*
> *your humble servant, set out on . . . my own money and*
> *my own traveling expenses, and received no salary what-*
> *soever from you, great Sovereign, either in cash or grain*
> *or salt from 1642 to 1661. And last year, in 1661, . . .*
> *[I received] salt payment for the period of 1642 to 1661*
> *from your Majesty's treasury, but I, Senka, did not receive*
> *your Majesty's cash and bread [grain] salary. . . . I have*
> *risked my life, suffered great wounds and shed my blood,*

suffered cold and great hunger, and starved. And being in
that service, I was impoverished by piracy and incurred
heavy debts beyond my ability to repay, and am now
perishing in these debts.

Merciful Majesty, Tsar and Grand Duke Aleksei
Mikhailovich . . . grant me, your humble servant, for my
service to your Majesty and for my fervor [eager desire]
and for my hostages, and for my wounds and for the blood
and the piracy, and for all I had to suffer the full amount
of the salary due me in grain and money for the past years
from 1642 to 1661, lest I, your humble servant, be
tortured to death in shackling debts and be unable to
continue serving your Majesty, and finally perish.

Dezhnev had other reasons for complaint. During the course of his explorations, he discovered the Bering Strait, the body of water between Asia and Alaska. Unfortunately, he never received credit for his find, because a government official mislaid his report. Vitus Bering, a Danish explorer employed by the tsar, rediscovered the strait eighty years later, and it was named for him.

Glossary

autocrat: Someone with absolute power.

blasphemous: Insulting to God.

deacon: A church official.

epic: A long poem dealing with heroic events.

exile: Far away, often out of the country.

icon: A religious picture, usually painted on a small wooden panel.

keel: A wooden or metal piece that runs along the center of the bottom of a boat and helps keep it balanced.

lathe: A machine in which a piece of wood, ivory, or metal is spun around while a cutting tool shapes it.

lay: A song.

Lent: The forty-day period of penitence and fasting before Easter.

pagan: Someone who is not a Christian, a Jew, or a Muslim.

peasant: A worker on the land.

pike: A long spear.

regent: Someone who governs a kingdom during the period when the rightful ruler is too young, or unable, to take command.

serf: A peasant bound to a lord or the Church.

streltsy: The musketeers who guarded Moscow.

turner: A person who shapes objects with a lathe.

For Further Reading

McDermott, Kathleen. *Peter the Great*. New York: Chelsea House Publishers, 1991.

Moscow, Henry. *Russia under the Czars*. New York: American Heritage Publishing, 1962.

Putnam, Peter Brock. *Peter, The Revolutionary Tsar*. New York: Harper and Row, 1973.

Roberson, John R. *Transforming Russia, 1682 to 1991*. New York: Atheneum, 1992.

Schomp, Virginia. *Russia*. New York: Marshall Cavendish, 1996.

Bibliography

Anderson, M. S. *Peter the Great*. London: Thames and Hudson, 1978.

Baron, Samuel H., ed. *The Travels of Olearius in Seventeenth-Century Russia*. Stanford: Stanford University Press, 1967.

Blum, Jerome. *Lord and Peasant in Russia*. Princeton, NJ: Princeton University Press, 1961.

Ehre, Milton, ed. *The Theater of Nikolay Gogol*. Chicago: University of Chicago Press, 1980.

Florinsky, Michael T. *Russia: A Short History*. New York: Macmillan, 1969.

Grey, Ian. *The Horizon History of Russia*. New York: American Heritage Publishing, 1970.

Guerney, Bernard G. *A Treasury of Russian Literature.* New York: Vanguard Press, 1943.

Hughes, Lindsey. *Russia in the Age of Peter the Great.* New Haven, CT: Yale University Press, 1998.

Kozlow, Jules. *The Kremlin.* New York: Thomas Nelson and Sons, 1958.

Lincoln, W. Bruce. *The Conquest of a Continent: Siberia and the Russians.* New York: Random House, 1994.

———. *The Romanovs.* New York: Dial Press, 1981.

Massie, Robert K. *Peter the Great.* New York: Alfred A. Knopf, 1980.

Oliva, L. Jay, ed. *Peter the Great.* Englewood Cliffs, NJ: Prentice-Hall, 1970.

Pipes, Richard. *Russia under the Old Regime.* New York: Macmillan, 1992.

Raeff, Marc. *Peter the Great Changes Russia.* 2d ed. Lexington, MA: D. C. Heath and Company, 1972.

Riasanovsky, Nicholas V. *A History of Russia.* 5th ed. New York: Oxford University Press, 1993.

Troyat, Henri. *Peter the Great.* New York: E. P. Dutton, 1987.

Vernadsky, George, ed. *A Source Book for Russian History from Early Times to 1917.* Vol. 1. New Haven, CT: Yale University Press, 1972.

Voyce, Arthur. *Moscow and the Roots of Russian Culture.* Norman, OK: University of Oklahoma Press, 1964.

Wallace, Robert. *Rise of Russia.* New York: Time-Life Books, 1967.

Weber, Friedrich Christian. *The Present State of Russia.* New York: Da Capo Press, 1968.

Zenkovsky, Serge A., ed. *Medieval Russia's Epics, Chronicles, and Tales.* New York: E. P. Dutton, 1974.

ON-LINE INFORMATION*

http://www.europe/hisruss.html
Russia at the time of Peter the Great. There are good links on this website.

http://www.interknowledge.com/russia/rushis04.html
An excellent index to resources on the time of Peter the Great.

*Websites change from time to time. For additional on-line information, check with the media specialist at your local library.

Index

Page numbers for illustrations are in **boldface**

Notes

Part One: The Tsar Who Transformed Russia

Page 27 "Soldiers: the hour has struck": Massie, *Peter the Great*, p. 489.
Page 28 "Money is the lifeblood": Hughes, *Russia in the Age of Peter the Great*, p. 494.
Page 31 "a city built on bones": Massie, *Peter the Great*, p. 361.
Page 33 "I will deprive you": Troyat, *Peter the Great*, p. 208.

Part Two: Everyday Life in Tsarist Russia

Page 49 "The church is near": Wallace, *Rise of Russia*, p. 137.
Page 61 "A good wife": Lincoln, *The Romanovs*, p. 83.

Part Three: The Russians in Their Own Words

Page 66 "Thus Oleg ruled": Zenkovsky, *Medieval Russia's Epics, Chronicles, and Tales*, pp. 53–54.
Page 67 "drink is the joy": Riasanovsky, *A History of Russia*, p. 35.
Page 68 "The envoys reported": Grey, *The Horizon History of Russia*, p. 40.
Page 69 "Igor spoke to his warriors": Zenkovsky, *Medieval Russia's Epics, Chronicles, and Tales*, pp. 170–179.
Page 71 "Punish your son": Vernadsky, *A Source Book for Russian History from Early Times to 1917*, p. 164.
Page 71 "Enjoin your servants": Wallace, *Rise of Russia*, p. 139.
Page 72 "Where there are no fish": Guerney, *A Treasury of Russian Literature*, p. 1043.
Page 72 "Tsar Ivan was physically unattractive": Zenkovsky, *Medieval Russia's Epics, Chronicles, and Tales*, pp. 388–390.
Page 74 "I, your humble servant": Grey, *The Horizon History of Russia*, p. 144.